Letter From The Founder

ANISA CRESPO

Co-Founder, Million Dollar Mom Society

Dear Radiant Readers,

Welcome to your Summer of Success—a season for thriving, realigning, and rising into the women we were always meant to be.

As the sun stretches longer in the sky and the days become warmer, we are given a beautiful opportunity for a mid-year reset. June marks the halfway point of the year—a moment to pause, reflect, and reignite. Whether you've hit every goal you set in January or life has taken you down a detour (or ten), now is your time to breathe deeply, reset your vision, and recommit to your growth.

This month's issue is all about cultivating success on your own terms. It's not just about business wins or checking boxes on your to-do list. It's about embracing your journey as a whole woman—bold, brilliant, and beautifully complex. Whether you're building an empire, finding your voice, starting over, or simply learning to rest and receive, this edition is for YOU.

Inside, you'll find powerful growth strategies, mid-year planning tools, and inspiring stories from women who are leading with both fire and grace. These are the kind of women who remind us that success isn't just a destination—it's a lifestyle. One rooted in authenticity, alignment, and community.

This season, I encourage you to soak in the sun-kissed inspiration around you. Get outside. Dream a little louder. Say yes to the thing you've been putting off. Maybe that means launching the business, pivoting your brand, taking a weekend away for yourself, or finally asking for the support you need. You don't have to hustle yourself into burnout to be worthy of success. You can thrive with ease, joy, and purpose.

The Million Dollar Mom Society has always been about more than just moms. It's about women—women who dare to rise, who lead with heart, and who are ready to rewrite the narrative for what's possible. If you're reading this, I want you to know: there's room for you at the table. You belong here. And your voice, your vision, and your victory matters.

Let this be your reminder that you are allowed to evolve. You are allowed to reset your goals, change direction, and choose joy. You are allowed to take up space, speak your truth, and shine—unapologetically.
As we step into this radiant new season, I invite you to embrace the warmth, the wildness, and the wisdom within you. The world needs your light.

With sunlit love and fierce belief in your journey,

Anisa Crespo
Co-Founder, *Million Dollar Mom Society*

Letter From The Founder

NATOSHA NAVARRO

Co-Founder, Million Dollar Mom Society

Hello Beautiful Souls,

As we step into this vibrant Summer of Success, I want you to take a moment—right here, right now—and ask yourself: What do I really want the second half of this year to feel like?

So often, we're so busy doing, serving, creating, and surviving that we forget to pause and check in with ourselves. But June is your sacred checkpoint. A chance to reset. A chance to realign. A chance to thrive.
This issue is your invitation to do just that.

Whether you're a mama in the thick of nap schedules and Zoom calls, a woman chasing her dreams while juggling a day job, or someone finally stepping into her own light after years of putting others first—this magazine was made with YOU in mind.

I know firsthand how easy it is to lose ourselves in the hustle. I'm a mom of two boys under four, a wife, and an entrepreneur who wears many hats. And let me tell you—it's not always graceful. But what I've learned is this: success doesn't require perfection. It requires presence. Progress. And a whole lot of self-compassion.

This summer, I want you to stop waiting for the *"perfect time"* and start honoring the powerful woman you already are. Inside this issue, you'll find practical tools for a mid-year reset, mindset shifts that create real momentum, and stories from women who are courageously carving their own path in life and business.

We are not just building brands or side hustles—we are building legacies. We are rewriting the script for what's possible, not only for ourselves, but for the next generation watching us. That's the heart behind the Million Dollar Mom Society. It's not about having it all together. It's about having a community that lifts you while you figure it out.

So, take the leap. Book the call. Launch the offer. Say the prayer. Take the nap. Whatever thriving looks like for you right now, lean into that. Your journey is unfolding exactly as it's meant to, and I am so proud of you for continuing to show up.

Thank you for being part of this mission. Thank you for pouring into yourself, your dreams, and this sisterhood. I believe this summer is going to be a turning point for so many of us—and I can't wait to see you rise.

With love and fierce encouragement,

Natosha Navarro
Co-Founder, *Million Dollar Mom Society*

MILLION DOLLAR
Mom Society
The
SOCIETY

WHERE AMBITIOUS WOMEN LIKE YOU RISE TO THE NEXT LEVEL

No more hustle without results. No more figuring it out alone. It's time to rise—with strategy, clarity, and a sisterhood that actually gets it.

The Society is your space to grow, lead, and thrive. You'll get direct access to expert mentorship, powerful business trainings, and a high-level community of women who are serious about success.

Imagine waking up each day with a clear plan, a support system in your corner, and the tools to turn followers into clients—and goals into real results. You're not meant to play small. You're meant to scale with purpose, confidence, and impact.

JOIN THE MOVEMENT www.milliondollarmom.org/thesocietymdms

From Struggle to Success:
Why Your Past Doesn't Define Your Future

By Cindy Witteman

If someone had told me years ago that I would be here today, running a successful business, inspiring others, and living a life of purpose, I might have laughed in disbelief. Not because I didn't dream of something more, but because I had been conditioned to believe that success was for other people.

People who came from wealth.
People who had the right connections.
People who had a smooth start in life.

I wasn't one of those people. I grew up super poor. I am a domestic violence survivor, which forced me into single parenthood. My story began with obstacles, struggle, and a long road of setbacks. But I am here to tell you something I learned along the way. Your past does not define you. Your story of origin does not dictate your success.

If you have a dream inside of you, no matter where you come from, you can turn it into a reality.

The Power of a Decision
For a long time, I felt trapped by my circumstances. I looked around and thought, "this is just how life is." But somewhere inside of me, I knew I was meant for more, despite not knowing what that meant or how to figure out what to do to achieve it. I was carrying the weight of self-doubt, fear, and the belief that I wasn't meant for more. But the moment I decided to rewrite my story, everything changed.

It did not happen overnight. There was no magic formula. Just a decision to refuse to be a victim of my past, a decision to take control of my future, a decision to push forward even when the odds were stacked against me.

That is what success is. Not luck. Not perfect timing. Just a series of decisions to keep going, even when it is hard.

Turning Obstacles into Opportunities
I wish I could tell you that once I decided to change my life, everything magically fell into place. But that is not how success works. Every time I stepped forward, there were new challenges.

I did not have a financial safety net.
I did not have a blueprint for success.
I did not even know where to start.
I did not even know anyone who was even moderately successful. I did not even know what being successful looked like. But I knew I wanted to find out.

Instead of focusing on what I lacked, I focused on what I could do. I learned. I adapted. I failed and got back up. Each setback became a lesson. Each "no" became fuel to find a "yes."

Obstacles will always be there. The question is, will you let them stop you, or will you turn them into opportunities?

Believing in the Power of Possibility
One of the hardest things about breaking through to success is believing that it is possible for you. Not just for the people you see on magazine covers or the women who seem to have it all figured out, but for you.

There were days when I doubted myself. Days when I wanted to quit. But every time I felt that pull to give up, I reminded myself why I started.

I was not just building success for myself.

I was building it to show my daughters, to show others, especially other women and moms, that it can be done.

And here is what I want to tell you: If I can do it, so can you.

You do not need to have all the answers. You do not need to wait for the perfect moment. You just need to start.

Your Success Story Starts Now

No matter where you come from, no matter what your past looks like, you have the power to create a future beyond what you ever imagined.

You are not your struggles.
You are not your failures.
You are not the person people doubted.

You are capable. You are powerful. You are worthy of success.

Along the way, I achieved milestones that still humble me today. In 2017, I started the nonprofit Driving Single Parents, where we give away cars to single parents in need. I authored five best-selling books. In 2023, I launched the Little Give TV Show, where we highlight ordinary people doing extraordinary things to help others. I am also the Founder and Editor-in-Chief of Force Magazine, where we celebrate individuals who are a force to be reckoned with. If I can build it from the ground up, then you can become a Million Dollar Mom too!

I know this because I have lived it. And now, I am here to tell you, it is your turn.

Please feel free to reach out and connect, I love connecting with like minded individuals.

VISIT
FORCEMAGAZINEFEATURE.COM

Connect With Cindy
www.CindyWitteman.com

DRIVING
Single Parents
DrivingSingleParents.org

Summer of Success:
Thrive in Business & Life This Season

by Jacqueline Crider

Ah, summer—the season of longer days, spontaneous adventures, and for mompreneurs, an ever-evolving schedule that can feel like a juggling act. Between client calls, summer camps, and the "Mom, I'm bored" chorus on repeat, keeping your business and financial goals on track might seem impossible.

But here's the truth: Summer isn't a season to stall—it's a season to reset, realign, and thrive.

This isn't about cramming in more work or feeling guilty for slowing down. It's about using this season to reconnect with what truly moves the needle —both financially and personally. And that's where the Financial Instinct Framework (FIF) comes in. When you align your financial and business strategies with your natural instincts, success feels effortless, not exhausting.

Step 1: Mid-Year Reset - What's Actually Working?
Think of your financial and business strategy like a GPS. If you don't check your route, you might end up way off track.

Ask yourself:
- What financial and business goals did I set at the start of the year?
- Are they still aligned with where I want to go?
- What's flowing effortlessly vs. what feels forced?

One of the biggest mistakes entrepreneurs make is sticking to a plan that no longer fits. Just because you set a goal in January doesn't mean it's the right one for July. Give yourself permission to pivot.

FIF Insight: Your financial instincts are always guiding you—are you listening? If something feels forced or draining, it's a sign to realign.

Step 2: Streamline & Simplify - Less Overwhelm, More Wealth
Summer is the season of simplicity. Let's apply that to your finances and business.
- Audit Your Offers & Expenses – What's actually bringing revenue vs. what's just keeping you busy?
- Batch Your Work – Whether it's content creation, sales calls, or financial planning, do it in focused bursts so you can enjoy more summer freedom.
- Leverage Passive & Recurring Income – Can you package up existing knowledge into a course, membership, or template?

FIF Insight: Wealth isn't built through nonstop hustle—it's built through smart, aligned choices.

Step 3: The Power of Visibility - Stay Top of Mind Without Burnout
Just because you take a step back doesn't mean your business has to disappear.
- Create Magnetic Content in Advance – Repurpose high-performing posts from earlier this year (new eyes = new engagement).
- Show Your Summer Freedom – Share behind-the-scenes moments that align with your brand message.
- Nurture, Don't Just Sell – Use storytelling to connect, not just promote. Your audience wants to see you thriving.

FIF Insight: Trust that consistency looks different in different seasons. Showing up doesn't always mean pushing sales—it means staying connected.

Step 4: Growth Strategies That Align With Your Financial Blueprint
Instead of overloading your summer with work, focus on strategic growth.
- Leverage Collaborations – Tap into new audiences through joint ventures, guest spots, or strategic partnerships.
- Optimize Pricing & Offers – Is your pricing still aligned with the value you provide? Now's a great time to adjust for profitability.
- Plant Seeds for Q4 – Summer may be slower for sales, but it's the perfect time to prep for a strong finish to the year.

FIF Insight: Success isn't about doing more—it's about aligning your efforts with your financial instincts.

Step 5: Sun-Kissed Mindset & Financial Freedom

Success isn't just about what's in your bank account—it's about how you feel while building it.

- Protect Your Non-Negotiables – What do you need to feel financially and personally fulfilled this summer? More time with family? More time off? Prioritize it.
- Celebrate Wins (Even Small Ones!) – Shift your focus from "not enough" to recognizing how far you've come.
- Embody the Wealth You Want – What would your next-level self do this summer? Lean into those decisions now.

FIF Insight: Your financial future is shaped by how you operate today. Small, aligned choices create long-term wealth.

Final Thought: Your Success, Your Terms

The biggest lesson of summer? You don't have to do business like everyone else. The Financial Instinct Framework is built on the belief that true financial freedom comes when you trust yourself, break the rules that don't fit, and build a wealth strategy that aligns with your unique strengths.

This summer, choose to thrive. Choose to reset, simplify, and step into the second half of the year with confidence, ease, and an unstoppable mindset.

Ready to align your finances and business with what actually works for YOU? Let's make it happen. Scan the QR code to find out what is your financial spirit animal!

Connect With Jacqueline

www.pbjteam.com
www.facebook.com/pbjmortgage

Creating Your Legacy in Every Moment

by Nikki Hillhouse

A meaningful legacy is not built on material achievements but on the values and choices we pass on. It is demonstrated through everyday actions —choosing self-worth over fear, advocating for ourselves and others, and aligning our lives with our core beliefs.

For me, legacy is not just about my professional work but also about the example I set for my son and my clients. I want my son to witness resilience in action, understanding that setbacks don't define us; it's how we rise from them that shapes who we are. Through embodying strength, compassion, and self-care, I aim to teach him and my clients that true power lies not in avoiding challenges, but in how we face them and respond. By living these values, I hope to inspire both my son and my clients to embrace their own resilience and step into their fullest potential.

Legacy is built through daily decisions and consistent actions. Living in alignment with core values sets a strong example for future generations. Resilience and self-empowerment influence those around us.

Embracing Growth Over Perfection

Perfection is an illusion that often prevents progress. True growth comes from embracing challenges, learning from failures, and continuously evolving. I transformed my struggles into lessons that now fuel my coaching business and wellness retreats, helping others find their own path to healing.

A growth mindset fosters resilience by shifting focus from setbacks to opportunities for learning. When we view challenges as stepping stones rather than barriers, we cultivate inner strength and adaptability. This shift allows us to take action with confidence, even in uncertain situations.

Perfection is not the goal; growth is.
Every challenge offers an opportunity to learn and evolve.
A resilient mindset leads to long-term transformation.

Owning your own Story

What kind of legacy are you creating? Are you reinforcing fear and self-doubt, or are you demonstrating courage and resilience? The impact we leave is shaped by how we live, the kindness we extend, and the way we inspire others.

The world needs more people who rise above adversity, reclaim their power, and create positive change. Your story is still being written, and every decision you make contributes to the legacy you build. The more you lean into your strength, the more you inspire those around you to do the same.

Our legacy is crafted by the choices we make, not the circumstances we face. Living with purpose and intention leaves a lasting mark. Every individual holds the power to transform their story and inspire those around them.

I won't let my past define who I am. I am dedicated to creating a future that is brighter and stronger.

Steps to Strengthen Your Legacy

1. Identify an area where you feel stuck – Reflect on what is holding you back and explore ways to move forward.
2. Take one small, proactive step – Whether it's learning something new, making a change in your routine, or reaching out for support, small actions add up.
3. Define the values you want to pass on – Write them down and practice embodying them in your daily life.
4. Shift your mindset from seeking perfection to embracing growth – Accept that mistakes and setbacks are part of the journey.
5. Make a commitment to live with courage and resilience – Choose to show up fully, even when things feel uncertain.

You were never meant to settle for mediocrity. This is your time to rise above limitations, embrace your unique journey, and take bold steps toward the life you were always meant to live step forward with confidence, shape a legacy that leaves an impact, and become a beacon of strength and inspiration for others to follow.

Connect With Nikki

www.nikkihillhouse.com
www.instagram.com/nikkihillhouse
www.facebook.com/nikki.hillhouse.1
www.linkedin.com/in/nikki-hillhouse-a6b25529b

Diva
NETWORK

READY TO LEAD, LAUNCH & LIVE LIKE A DIVA?

You've got the vision. Now you need the sisterhood, strategy, and support to scale it.

Welcome to **The Diva Network**—the ultimate business accelerator for bold women building profitable, passion-filled empires.

Get weekly networking, game-changing trainings, luxury travel perks, and real collaboration (minus the guru fluff and mean girl vibes).

Whether you're launching your first offer or ready for your founder's escape trip—we've got your seat at the table.

Join the network that's redefining what business should feel like. Start for just $112/month!

JOIN TODAY!

https://app.jointhedivas.com/ref/anisacrespo331?p=lp

My Journey with Hyperemesis Gravidarum and Postpartum Anxiety:
Why Automating Your Business is Essential for Mompreneurs

by Kelsi Taylor

Being a mompreneur is a challenging yet rewarding journey. But when you add the struggles of hyperemesis gravidarum and postpartum anxiety and depression to the mix, the challenges can feel insurmountable. As someone who has navigated these treacherous waters, I want to share my personal experience and highlight why automating your business can be a lifesaver for mompreneurs.

Battling Hyperemesis Gravidarum

Hyperemesis gravidarum (HG) is not your typical morning sickness. It's a severe condition that can make pregnancy feel like an endless struggle. For me, it meant constant nausea, frequent vomiting, and an inability to keep food or water down. Days blurred into weeks, and I found myself bedridden, grappling with the physical and emotional toll of this condition.

The Onset of Postpartum Anxiety and Depression

After the birth of my child, I hoped for a respite. However, I was soon confronted with postpartum anxiety and, later, depression. The overwhelming sense of responsibility, coupled with sleepless nights and the physical recovery from childbirth, made it difficult to manage my emotions. The anxiety was relentless, and depression cast a shadow over what should have been one of the happiest times of my life.

The Struggle of Balancing Business and Motherhood

As a mompreneur, my business is not just a job; it's a passion and a source of income. However, during my battle with HG and postpartum anxiety and depression, even the simplest tasks felt impossible. The pressure to maintain my business while taking care of a baby and dealing with my health issues was immense.

The Turning Point: Embracing Automation

The turning point in my journey came when I started therapy and decided to automate parts of my business. Here's how automation became my lifeline:

1. Time Management

Automation tools helped me manage my time more effectively. Scheduling software allowed me to plan social media posts, email campaigns, and blog updates. This meant that even on my worst days, my business continued to run smoothly.

2. Customer Relationship Management

CRM systems automated my customer interactions. From sending personalized emails to tracking customer behavior, these tools ensured that my clients felt valued and engaged without me being constantly available.

3. Financial Management

Automated invoicing and bookkeeping tools helped keep my finances in order. I could track expenses, send invoices, and monitor cash flow without the stress of manual calculations and paperwork.

4. Task Delegation

Automation allowed me to delegate tasks more efficiently. Virtual assistants and freelancers became an integral part of my business, handling tasks that didn't require direct involvement. This delegation was crucial in maintaining the quality of my services.

The Benefits of Automation for Mompreneurs

1. Reduced Stress: Automation reduces the day-to-day stress of managing a business. Knowing that key aspects of your business are running smoothly allows you to focus on your health and your family.
2. Increased Productivity: With repetitive tasks automated, you can focus on strategic planning and creative work, driving your business forward even when you're not at your best.
3. Better Work-Life Balance: Automation helps create a healthier work-life balance. It ensures that your business doesn't demand your constant attention, allowing you to spend more quality time with your family.
4. Consistency: Automation ensures consistency in your business operations. Whether it's posting on social media or sending newsletters, automation maintains a steady presence for your brand.

Conclusion

My journey with hyperemesis gravidarum and postpartum anxiety and depression taught me the importance of self-care and the value of efficient business management. Automation became the cornerstone of maintaining and growing my business during these challenging times. For all the mompreneurs out there, embracing automation can make a huge difference, allowing you to focus on what truly matters: your health and your family.

If you're struggling with similar challenges, know that you're not alone. Seek help, prioritize self-care, and consider automation as a tool to lighten your load. Your well-being and your business will both thrive as a result.

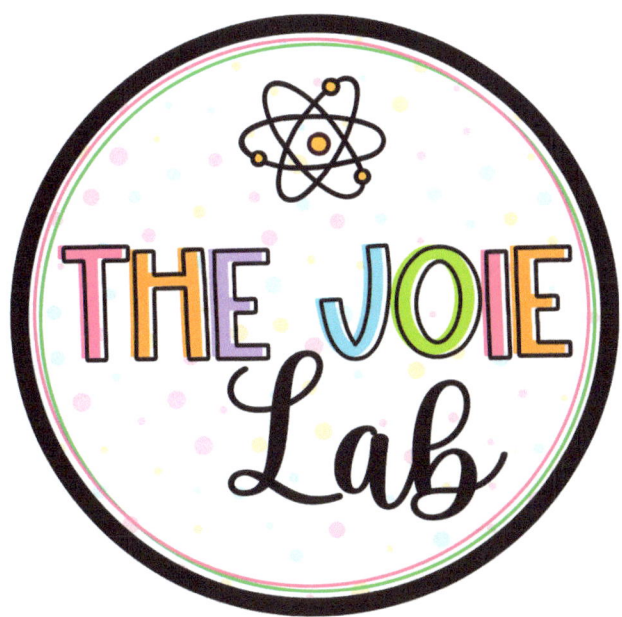

Connect With Kelsi

www.instagram.com/thejoielab
www.createjoie.com

Thriving Through the Unexpected:
My Journey to Motherhood and the Power of a Holistic Approach

by Alana Morris

Everything shifted after a school trip to Central America. Not enough older students had signed up, so they opened it to younger ones. I was 16 when I went — and what I experienced there changed my entire perspective. I returned home with a new awareness, a deeper appreciation for life, and an open heart to what the world had to offer.

At 26, after working a ski season abroad, I returned to my hometown to regroup financially before heading off on another adventure. But then I met my partner. I still travelled — to Thailand this time — and he joined me. We later bought a home and decided it was time to start a family.

But life had other plans.

Our fertility journey wasn't simple. It stretched on for years. I gave birth at 37 after facing more bumps in the road than I ever anticipated. Along the way, I met people who shared knowledge that completely changed my understanding of my body and health — none of it came from a doctor. I discovered how stress, toxins, nutrition, and emotional wellbeing all play powerful roles in fertility.

That's when I truly embraced a holistic approach. I learned how important it is to nourish the body, mind, and spirit — and how vital it is to feel empowered in your own journey. I wish I'd known then what I know now.

So I created The Fertility Sanctuary, a supportive Facebook group for women who are navigating their own fertility paths. It's a safe, heart-centered space to feel seen, supported, and guided — because no one should walk this road alone.

This summer, as we talk about thriving in life and business, let's not forget the quiet, powerful success of healing, growing, and believing in what's possible. If you're on a fertility journey, know that your story matters — and you're not alone.

Join me at The Fertility Sanctuary.

With love and belief in your journey,
Alana Morris

Like so many women, I spent my late teens and early twenties doing everything in my power not to get pregnant. I took the pill, had the injection, tried the implant — basically, anything the doctor suggested. We're told to wait until we have the perfect relationship, financial stability, a home, and a successful career before we even think about having children.

But here's the thing — deep down, I always wanted to be a mum. I remember my mum asking me when I was 14 what I wanted to do with my life. At the time, I was babysitting regularly and absolutely adored being around children. Without hesitation, I told her, "I'm going to be a mum... as soon as I'm 17." As you can imagine, she wasn't thrilled with that plan.

Connect With Alana

www.facebook.com/groups/24197563709844014

Divine Timing and Daily Discipline:
The Summer Strategy I Swear By

By Anisa Crespo, Co-Founder of Million Dollar Mom Society

Summer always brings with it a special kind of energy—light, warmth, freedom, and the undeniable pull to slow down and soak it all in. But for me, it's also a sacred time to tune in, get intentional, and align my life and business with both purpose and power.

People often ask me how I've managed to create multiple income streams from home, stay grounded in my faith, raise a family, and build a thriving community of women. The truth is, it's not just strategy—it's divine timing and daily discipline. One without the other is incomplete.

I used to live in a space of constant hustle—chasing opportunities, burning out, questioning my worth, and wondering if I was "too late." But once I surrendered to God's plan, everything began to shift. I realized that success wasn't something I had to force. It was something I had to align with.

Divine Timing Is Real

If you're in a season where things feel slow, stuck, or uncertain, I want to gently remind you: it's not a delay—it's divine timing. Some doors don't open because they're not meant to. Others swing wide only when we're truly ready. And sometimes, the answer is not yet because God is protecting us or preparing us for something better.

The moment I started to trust that the universe—and more importantly, God—wasn't working against me but actually working for me, I could finally breathe. I could move forward with peace, knowing that everything I do is a seed. And just like in nature, seeds take time to sprout. But they will—if you nurture them with intention and consistency.

Daily Discipline is the Container for Your Calling

Now here's the part people don't love to hear—but need to: waiting on divine timing doesn't mean sitting still. It means showing up daily with discipline. For me, that looks like:

- Morning gratitude, prayer and meditation before I touch my laptop
- Setting focused intentions for the day (not just to-do lists, but heart-aligned goals)
- Eating nourishing foods that fuel my body and mind
- Moving my body daily—whether that's a strength workout, walk, or stretching in the sun
- Making space for "me time" to unplug, recharge, and reconnect with myself
- Carving out non-negotiable time for income-producing activities—even if it's just one hour
- Protecting my energy from distractions, comparison, and noise
- Prioritizing rest and replenishment without guilt

Discipline doesn't mean rigidity. It means structure that serves your spiritual freedom. It's the foundation that allows miracles to land.

My Summer Strategy

This summer, I'm leaning into flow with focus. I create space for inspiration, but I also stick to the plan. I take aligned action, then I surrender the outcome. I ask God to guide my steps—and then I actually take those steps, even when they're uncomfortable.

If you're reading this, I want you to remember: you don't need a new year to start fresh. You just need a decision and a daily commitment to the woman you're becoming.

This is your Summer of Success. Let divine timing be your peace, and daily discipline be your power. The rest? It will unfold in the most beautiful, miraculous ways.

You've got this, sis.

With grace and grit,
Anisa Crespo

Connect With Anisa

www.facebook.com/anisacrespo
www.instagram.com/keepingupwiththecrespos
www.facebook.com/groups/milliondollarmomsociety
www.anisacrespo.com
www.milliondollarmom.org

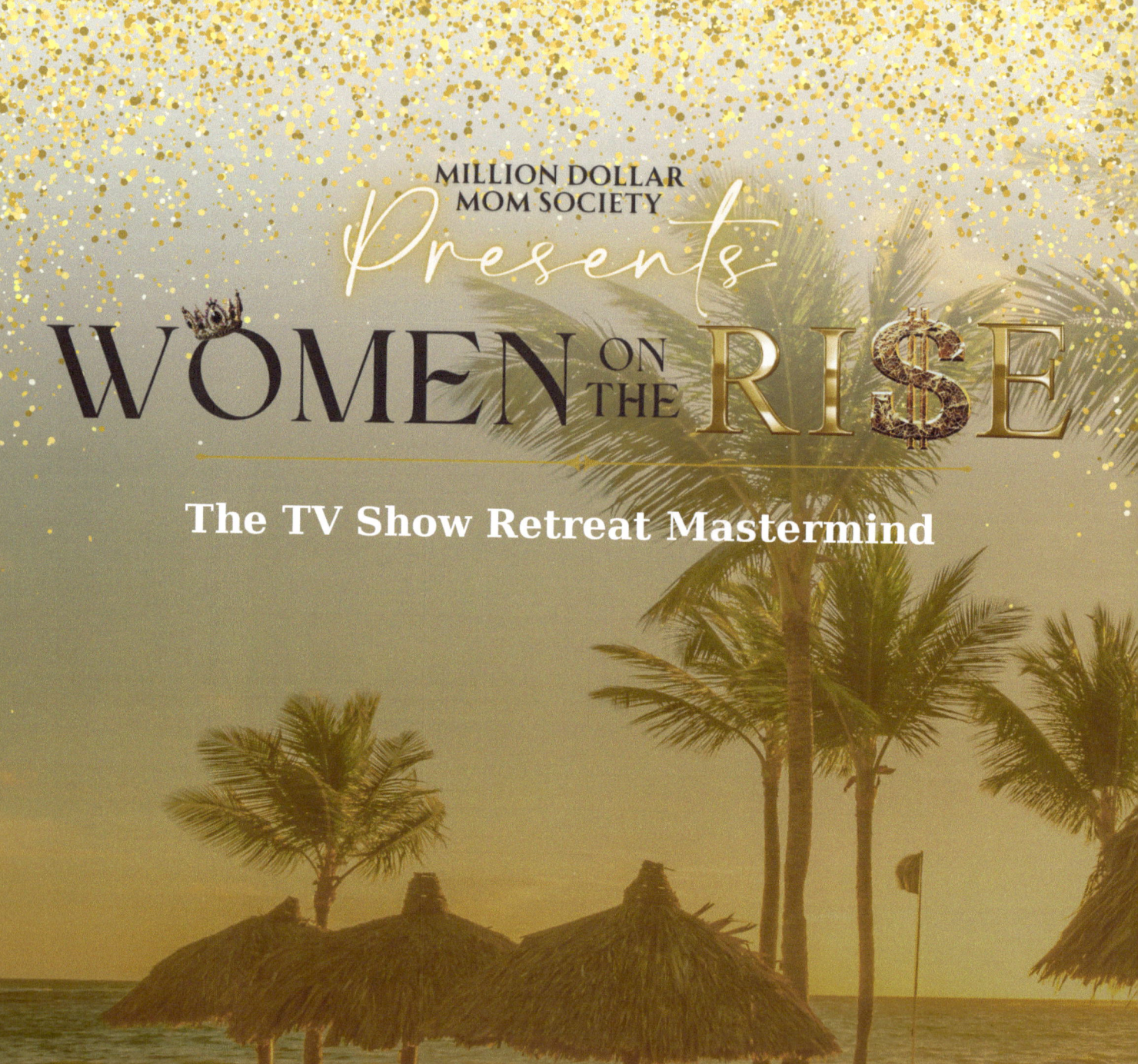

MILLION DOLLAR MOM SOCIETY

Presents

WOMEN ON THE RI$E

The TV Show Retreat Mastermind

A Luxury Experience for Visionary Women Entrepreneurs

November 9-12, 2025 | Laguna Beach, CA

Step into the spotlight with 50 powerhouse women ready to transform the world—and their businesses.

This isn't just another event.
It's a televised red carpet experience and mastermind, captured for a global docu-series on **Apple TV and major TV streaming platforms.**

Rub shoulders with celebrity speakers, elevate your brand on a world stage, and get the kind of visibility that turns leaders into legends.

Choose your tier of transformation—from **Rising Star** to **Spotlight**—and prepare for exclusive interviews, VIP dining, luxe accommodations, media exposure, spa indulgence, and unforgettable connections.

- Featuring **Forbes Riley**, Queen of the Perfect Pitch
- Hosted by **Million Dollar Mom Society Co-Founders**, Anisa Crespo & Natosha Navarro
- Filmed on-location at a breathtaking Laguna Beach resort

It's not about being seen.
It's about being remembered.

Apply Now and Claim Your Spotlight Before It's Gone.

www.milliondollarmom.org/womenontherise

YOUR RISE BEGINS THE MOMENT YOU SAY YES.

Mid-Year, Full Momentum:
My Simple System for Staying Focused and Fired Up

by Natosha Navarro, Co-Founder of Million Dollar Mom Society

Let's be honest—by the time summer hits, many entrepreneurs start losing steam. The goals we set in January? Some are thriving, others... well, they're buried under laundry, deadlines, and the chaos of everyday life. As a mom of two toddlers, wife, and multi-business owner, I know firsthand how easy it is to fall into survival mode.

But I also know this: mid-year isn't the time to slow down—it's the time to realign, reset, and reignite your momentum. You don't need to do more—you just need to do the right things, consistently.

Over the past few years, I've created a simple yet powerful system that keeps me focused, fired up, and in flow—even when life gets messy. And today, I'm sharing it with you, because I believe success is simple when you prioritize the things that actually move the needle.

1. Set Micro-Milestones

Forget the pressure of massive 12-month goals. Instead, break your year into 90-day sprints. Right now, I'm treating June through August as my "Summer of Strategy." I've chosen 3 core business goals and 2 personal goals to laser in on. Every week, I ask: What's one small action I can take that brings me closer to these?

Progress builds confidence—and confidence fuels momentum.

2. Protect Your Energy

As women, we give so much of ourselves—to our kids, our partners, our clients. But if your energy is constantly drained, your business will feel heavy. I'm intentional about morning routines that fuel me first: meditation, movement, hydration, and five minutes of quiet (yes, even if I have to hide in the bathroom to get it). I also limit unnecessary calls and say no to anything that doesn't align with my current season.

Energy is your most powerful currency—spend it wisely.

3. Use the Rule of Three

When life gets overwhelming, I go back to my Rule of Three:
- One thing that grows the business (a sales call, content creation, networking)
- One thing that strengthens the family (a fun activity, dinner with no distractions)
- One thing for myself (a workout, bath, massage, or a podcast in the car)

This keeps me grounded in what truly matters and helps me avoid burnout.

4. Don't Wait for Motivation—Create It

Let's be real: motivation isn't always there. I don't wake up every day feeling like a boss babe ready to conquer the world. But what I do have is discipline. I show up anyway. I've learned that the action comes before the feeling. When I do the thing—write the post, send the pitch, go live—I create momentum. And momentum creates motivation.

5. Build a Circle That Matches Your Commitment

Your circle will either fuel your fire or drain your dreams. I surround myself with women who are chasing goals, raising babies, and still showing up. That's the heart of the Million Dollar Mom Society—we rise together. You don't have to do this alone.

So if you're feeling behind or scattered halfway through the year, I want you to know: you're not off-track—you're right on time. This is your moment to reset, refocus, and reclaim your fire.

Let's finish this year strong—and sun-kissed.

With love and drive,
Natosha Navarro

Connect With Natosha

www.facebook.com/groups/milliondollarmomsociety
www.instagram.com/milliondollarmomsociety
www.facebook.com/100093980081725
www.milliondollarmom.org

Medicine For Your Body and Soul

by DK Hillard

Medicine is traditionally thought of as a drug prescribed by a doctor to treat a mental or physical ailment. In my spiritual practice, I have sought "other ways" to facilitate healing for myself and others—my own form of medicine.

"Western medicine" has saved my life before, so I don't discount its efficacy or importance in modern times, but pharmaceuticals and procedures have also wreaked havoc on my body. I've had the blessing and the curse of having health issues that Western medicine couldn't help, forcing me to dig deeper into what my body needs.

Many physical issues stem from an emotional imbalance, our body's way of signaling when we are out of whack. But decades of therapy weren't enough to bring my soul back to a healthy state. I needed to walk my true spiritual path and do the work of reclaiming my life.

Unfortunately, that was not enough either. After integrating all of the spiritual awakening and growth, I found myself sicker than ever, my body appearing to spiral rapidly downward, and bewildered.

During one painfully sleepless night I decided to turn to Spirit—going straight to the source for help. The message was clear: nothing thrives without love and I did not love my body—I have never loved it. The trauma of my childhood, though I thought I had long since "dealt with" it, had left me frozen. I had no unconditional love for this old, wrinkled body that was betraying my dreams and every attempt at fixing it. The truth was that I hadn't loved it even when it was in great shape.

This was about unconditional love for myself, my whole self. Not just my spirit, my soul, my essence, which I honored and cherished, but all of me including the physical vessel that housed it all. I had discounted the importance of that so many years ago that I was unaware of the impact it was having on my physical health. I was blind to the missing piece of my puzzle. Now I had to do the work of loving my physical self as well. That meant allowing myself to experience pleasure on a grander scale.

Physical sensation provides access to a deeper experience of yourself and to a path that transcends the mind and transports you beyond the present.

The feeling of bliss when we are touched in just the right way expands our energy, connecting us to our natural state of love, compassion and joy—we can feel the opening of our hearts. Some call this rapture. I call it living a full life, totally embodied as who I am, walking my true path. This can be a daily experience and not just something that happens once in a while.

I'm not alone here my friends. I'd say that most of us are living less than fully sensually aware lives. We live in a puritanical society that teaches us not to indulge in pleasure for pleasure's sake. Healing happens to the entirety of our being, the emotional, spiritual and the physical.

I've had to learn to live this way. It did not come naturally to me. We can all learn to live a more sensually aware life. The first step is to become aware of your resistance to feeling. Is it shame, embarrassment, a belief that it's bad? When you are aware of what's in the way, then you are free to make a choice. True vitality, health and abundance must include feeling free to feel all there is to feel in our body. After all, we are nature herself!

Connect With DK

www.dkhillard.com
www.dkhillardart.com
www.facebook.com/dkhillardwraptures
www.instagram.com/dkhillard
www.linkedin.com/in/debra-hillard-93526913

Finding Hope in Micro Moments:
Embracing a New Normal

by Erica Elliott

"What if this is as good as it gets?" The question haunted me as I lay on the couch, overwhelmed by a crushing migraine and fatigue. As a woman of faith, I've witnessed miracles, but after months of relentless pain, life felt unbearable. How could this be my reality?

I've always served others—as a counselor, coach, and in the military. Helping people has been my passion for over 30 years. Despite knowing others who lost their lives to COVID-19, I couldn't help but feel defeated. Each day became harder. The more I pushed, the worse I felt, a stark contrast to my military training, where persistence was the key to success.

When I contracted COVID-19 in November 2020, I didn't slow down. I kept working, helping clients cope with their issues. I told myself they needed me; I had no idea what that was doing to my body.

My optimism, usually my strength, began to crumble. I cried out to God, feeling lost. Doctors and Specialists —no one had answers. Diagnosed with Post Covid Syndrome hyperkalemia, migraines, hypothyroidism, adrenal fatigue and more, I was a shadow of my former self.

Then, everything began to change when I shifted my focus to small, manageable actions—what I now call micro steps.

The Power of Micro Moments

Accepting that pushing through wasn't the answer was difficult. Instead, I embraced micro steps—tiny actions taken in micro time. These small efforts allowed me to start rebuilding without overwhelming myself.

Here are a few strategies that helped me find hope:

1. Treat Yourself as a Friend: Be kind to yourself. If a friend were struggling, you wouldn't criticize them. The same goes for self-talk. Negative thoughts only make things worse.
2. Seek Divine Guidance: I asked God for direction, and solutions began to appear—new tools, supplements, or techniques that helped me move forward.
3. Advocate for Yourself: Doctors do their best with the knowledge they have, but it's crucial to keep searching until you find the right support. Don't settle—keep asking questions.
4. Micro Time Chunking: Break tasks into small time chunks. I set a timer for 15 minutes to work on a task, followed by a 30-45 minute rest. This approach helped my brain recognize success, boosting my spirits bit by bit.
5. Redefine Your Identity: You are not your diagnosis. Surround yourself with positive, encouraging people. Avoid groups that dwell on problems, as they can trap you in a cycle of negativity.
6. Get Out of the House: Even stepping outside for a few minutes can make a difference. Explore your surroundings, take mini-vacations, and break the monotony of being indoors.
7. Find a Mentor or Coach: We're not meant to navigate life alone. Having a counselor, coach, or mentor can be transformative.

Embracing the New Normal

Once I accepted that this might be as good as it gets, I found peace in micro moments. Micro time chunking, micro learning, and micro healing became the foundation of my new normal. Like someone recovering from a stroke, I learned to find joy, fulfillment, and purpose again, one tiny step at a time.

If you're struggling, know that hope exists in the smallest of moments. By embracing micro steps, you can create a life that's fulfilling, even if it looks different from what you once knew. The key is to settle into this new norm and find bliss in the micro moments. Little by little, you'll discover that even if this is as good as it gets, it can still be good.

Connect With Erica

www.linkedin.com/in/erica-elliott-ms-lpc-b90911150
www.facebook.com/warriorheartxo
www.instagram.com/warriorheartxo
www.msha.ke/warriorheartxo
www.linktr.ee/WarriorHeartxo

"You have breast cancer."

by Beth Burniche

Until you hear those words spoken to you, it's hard to grasp the weight they carry. In an instant, life divides: before and after. Mine changed again two weeks later when I learned the cancer had spread to my bones. I was Stage 4—metastatic breast cancer.

My first thought wasn't about treatment. It was my one-year-old son. I thought, I won't see him start kindergarten. After all we went through to have a child, the idea of missing so much was crushing.

As an independent beauty consultant, I was used to planning, figuring things out. But this was different. Everything felt out of my hands.

What I've Learned

Here's what I wish more people knew: Stage 4 breast cancer isn't always the death sentence it once was. Thanks to advances in medicine, many of us live with it as a chronic illness. When one treatment stops working, we often have others to try. But that future depends on research—and the funding behind it.

Only 2–5% of breast cancer research focuses on Stage 4. That's despite it being the only stage that's terminal. Organizations like METAvivor (https://metavivor.org/) are working to change that.

Every day, 115 people in the U.S. die from metastatic breast cancer. That's 115 mothers, daughters, partners—leaders—gone daily.

Advocacy Is a Business Skill, Too

In 2025, critical cancer research funding from both the National Institutes of Health and the Congressionally Directed Medical Research Programs (CDMRP) was cut. That means fewer trials, fewer treatments, and slower progress—especially for metastatic breast cancer.

As women who lead, build, and influence, we have the power to help. Use your voice and platform. Call your representatives. Donate or raise funds. Support organizations like METAvivor or the American Cancer Society (https://www.cancer.org/), which provides transportation, lodging, and other vital services to patients.

How to Support People Living with Stage 4

Support also means seeing us as whole people—not just "fighters" or "survivors." Most of us don't want to be called heroes. We're still who we were before cancer, just navigating life with more weight.

If someone in your life is living with metastatic cancer, ask how you can help in specific ways. Say, "Would it help if I picked up groceries?" or "Can I handle school pickup this week?" That's much easier than leaving it to us to ask—which we often won't, because we already feel like a burden.

Everyone's needs are different, but easing someone's daily load—childcare, errands, meals—makes a real difference. So does treating us with normalcy, humor, and respect.

Looking Forward

Today, I'm preparing to watch my son finish second grade—blowing past that kindergarten milestone I thought I'd never see. I've met people living 10, 20, even 30 years with metastatic breast cancer. I fully plan to be one of them.

To the women reading this—whether you're running a company, a household, or both—know this: your leadership can extend beyond your business. It can shape policy, fund research, and build a world where more of us live longer, fuller lives with cancer.

Metastatic breast cancer is a lifelong negotiation. But with research, compassion, and community, it doesn't have to be a life cut short.

Connect With Beth

www.marykay.com/bburniche
www.facebook.com/groups/GreatSkinCare

Your Success Isn't Just About Strategy —It's About Nervous System Safety

by Monica Connolly

There comes a moment in every woman's journey when she realizes the success she's chasing no longer feels fulfilling. She has the titles, the calendar full of clients, maybe even the dream business she once prayed for—yet something feels off. Her energy is drained. Her body feels heavy. Her spark has dimmed.

As a mom, entrepreneur, and transformation coach, I know that feeling all too well. And what I've come to realize—both through my personal story and through coaching dozens of high-achieving women—is that strategy can only take you so far. True, lasting success isn't built on hustle alone. It's built on healing. Specifically, nervous system healing.

Let's talk about the piece most women are missing.

You're Not Failing—You're Dysregulated

If you're waking up tired even after eight hours of sleep...
If you can't stop emotionally eating or overthinking every decision...
If your mind is spinning with to-dos but your body feels frozen...
That's not laziness. It's not a lack of discipline.
It's nervous system dysregulation.

When we've spent years in survival mode—balancing caregiving, business, and everyone else's needs—our bodies learn to operate from fight, flight, freeze, or fawn. We become addicted to the hustle and disconnected from our own needs. We overgive, overextend, and override our intuition. Over time, we stop feeling safe—inside our own bodies.

No amount of strategy will override a body that feels unsafe to succeed.

Regulated Women Rise

The game-changer? Learning to feel safe in your body again.

When you regulate your nervous system, you don't just feel better—you make decisions from clarity instead of chaos. You set boundaries without guilt. You attract aligned clients and opportunities because your energy is grounded, not frantic.

Regulation gives you access to the next level version of yourself—the one who doesn't shrink when the spotlight finds her. The one who shows up with confidence because she's rooted in peace, not performance.

Success becomes sustainable. Purpose becomes embodied.

Three Ways to Start Regulating Today

Breathe with Intention:
Before your next big decision or during a moment of stress, try box breathing—inhale for 4, hold for 4, exhale for 4, hold for 4. Do this for 1-2 minutes and feel your body return to center.

Feel Instead of Fix:
Notice your emotions instead of judging or numbing them. Ask yourself: What do I need right now? Learning to sit with discomfort instead of bypassing it is key to nervous system repair.

Create Micro Moments of Safety:
This could be sipping your favorite tea, stepping outside barefoot, journaling, or listening to calming music. These small acts tell your brain, "I'm safe," even when life feels overwhelming.

You Were Made for More—But You Can't Heal Alone
Let's be real: nervous system work isn't always easy, especially for women who are used to being the strong one. That's why community matters. That's why slowing down matters.

This summer, instead of adding more to your plate, ask yourself: Where can I soften? What if success isn't about doing more, but feeling safer in my own skin?

This is your permission slip to stop performing and start embodying success. Because you don't have to choose between ambition and alignment. You don't have to sacrifice your health or joy for the next milestone.

You get to have both.

Connect With Monica

www.monicaconnollycoaching.com
www.facebook.com/monica.a.connolly.7
www.instagram.com/monicaconnollyandco
www.linkedin.com/feed

Possibility to *Prosperity*

30 Powerful Journeys of Transforming Passion into Purpose

Possibility to Prosperity is an inspiring anthology by Anisa Crespo, Natosha Navarro, and 28 co-authors, sharing powerful stories of women who transformed passion into purpose-driven success. It celebrates perseverance, vision, and the limitless power of possibility.

The Possibility to Prosperity anthology package includes a professionally edited chapter, global publishing and distribution, custom book design, and comprehensive marketing support across major retailers and social media networks. Authors retain full ownership and royalties with the option to purchase copies at wholesale prices. This package ensures maximum visibility and impact for your story.

JOIN THE ANTHOLOGY NOW

WWW.MILLIONDOLLARMOM.ORG/POSSIBILITY_TO_PROSPERITY

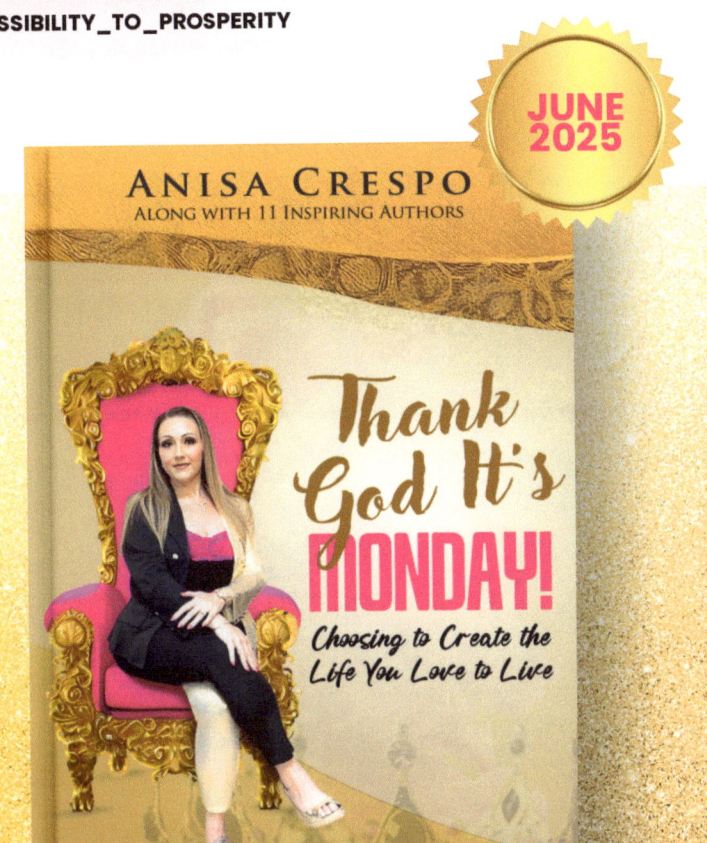

Exciting News!

We're thrilled to share
Thank God It's Monday, coming out June 2025!

This powerful anthology features inspiring stories from extraordinary women who have transformed their passions into purpose-driven success. Get ready to be motivated, empowered, and equipped to design a life you truly love.

Break Free:
How Purpose Unlocks the Chains of Fear

by Elizabeth Meigs

More than 70% of adults today report feeling stuck—trapped between where they are and where they long to be. In careers, in relationships, and even in the silent battles of the mind, stagnation often feels inevitable. I understand this because I've lived it. And through that journey, I discovered something vital: it isn't fear that holds us captive—it's the meaning we assign to it.

At just 14 years old, I had big dreams of becoming a country music star. But a devastating car accident shattered more than my physical body—it shattered my identity. I lost the voice that once defined me. I lost the vision I had for my future. Grief, judgment, and self-doubt became constant companions, and I often cried out, "Why me?"
In those darkest hours, a whisper arose—not from outside, but from deep within:
"I have a plan for you. You can't stop. You have to keep going."

That whisper didn't erase my fear. But it introduced something far more powerful: purpose. And purpose, I came to realize that purpose isn't just a feeling we stumble upon—it's a calling woven into our very design, a reflection of who we were created to become.

Too often, we see fear as a reason to stop. But when we take a closer look, we realize fear isn't the end—it's the beginning. It's a doorway to purpose, signaling that something greater is waiting just beyond our comfort zone.

When we lack this understanding, we give fear dominance. We allow old injuries, limiting beliefs, and unresolved doubts to shape our decisions without ever questioning their validity. But when we begin observing—truly observing—our experiences differently, fear becomes something else entirely: a catalyst for growth.

When I chose to pursue a career in Occupational Therapy, it wasn't because I had no fear—it was because I chose to assess my experiences differently. My injuries, once seen only as loss, became my greatest asset. They became a bridge of empathy, connection, and deep understanding for those I served.

Later, when faced with toxic environments, burnout, and the collapse of my marriage, I applied the same lens. I asked not "Why is this happening to me?" but "How is this rebuilding me?"
Each time, purpose pulled me forward—not away from fear, but through it.

Today, through the Pathway to PEACE Method™ and the Roadmap to Resilience™ framework, I coach women to reclaim their own stories—not by pretending fear doesn't exist, but by daring to assess it differently.

The goal isn't to eliminate fear. It's to reveal the truth:

You are not stuck because you're broken.
You are stuck because something inside you is ready to grow.

Pain, self-doubt, and fear are real. But they are not final. When you observe them with curiosity instead of judgment, you begin to see that every obstacle is building the resilience you will one day stand upon.

The greatest breakthrough comes when you dare to believe there is a purpose greater than fear could ever steal.
The chains that hold you are not stronger than the calling that beckons you.

This is not just motivation. It's a method. It's a call to dive into your story, your purpose, and the unshakable truth of who you were always meant to be.

You were created for more.

And everything you need to move forward is already within you.
The journey begins not when fear disappears, but when purpose becomes louder than your doubt.

It's time to move. It's time to rise.
It's time to step boldly into the life you were created for.

Connect With Elizabeth

www.elizabethinspires.com
www.elizabethinspires.com/pathway-to-peace
www.facebook.com/ElizabethMeigsInspires
www.instagram.com/elizabethmeigsinspires
www.linkedin.com/in/elizabethinspires

The Sacred Reset:
A 21-Day Journey to Heal, Reclaim, and Rise

by Tywanah Evette

Connect With Tywanah

www.blackbutterflygoddess.com
www.healHER.biz
www.facebook.com/BlackButterflyGoddess888
www.linkedin.com/in/blackbutterflygoddess
www.instagram.com/blackbutterflygoddess
www.tiktok.com/@blackbutterflygoddess

In honor of National PTSD Awareness Month, this daily email or Slack-based healing experience is helping women move from survival mode to sacred restoration—one prompt, one reflection, one brave breath at a time.

> "This isn't about fixing yourself— it's about remembering the wholeness that's always been within."
>
> —Tywanah Evette, Creator of The Sacred Reset

June marks National PTSD Awareness Month—a time to shine light on the invisible wounds so many women carry. For survivors of trauma, healing isn't linear or fast. It's often quiet, internal, and filled with questions like, Will I ever feel safe again? Will I ever feel like myself? This is the heartbeat behind The Sacred ResetTM—a 21-day guided journey created for women who are ready to move out of survival and into sacred healing.

The Sacred Reset delivers daily doses of nourishment through beautifully written email prompts, reflections, and healing activities, helping women reconnect to themselves in body, mind, and spirit. Each day's message is intentionally crafted to guide participants through emotional release, spiritual clarity, and nervous system restoration.

Whether it's a soul-deep journaling prompt, a simple grounding ritual, or a reflection that gently asks you to see your truth through a softer lens—this journey meets you where you are. There's no pressure to be perfect. Just an invitation to show up.

"Many of us don't even realize we're still operating in survival mode," says creator Tywanah Evette, a Spiritual Strategist and Trauma Recovery Facilitator. "We're functioning, working, parenting—but we've forgotten how to just be. This Reset is about rediscovering that. Gently. Daily. With love."

In a world that encourages women to push through pain, The Sacred Reset offers a sacred pause—and a powerful return.

Sidebar (callout box or separate section):

Join The Sacred ResetTM

Ready to begin your healing journey?

Sign up to receive:
- Daily emailed or Slack channel journaling prompts
- Spiritual reflections + affirmations
- Healing activities for nervous system reset
- A safe container for emotional release and soul reconnection

Register at: https://stan.store/BlackButterflyGoddess/p/the-sacred-reset
Start Date: June 1st, 2025 (or your chosen launch date)
Space is limited to ensure a personal, sacred experience.

she wins

WOMEN'S NETWORK

Elevate your business with the power of community.

Get access to the tools, connections, and support you need to grow—with a circle of women who truly get it.

WHAT'S INCLUDED

- Strategic networking & mentorship
- Expert-led masterclasses & exclusive resources
- Member spotlights, VIP perks & more

Join for just

$87/MONTH

no contracts, cancel anytime.

www.shewinswomensnetwork.com

From $1.54 to Freedom:
How I Broke the Health & Wealth Curse as a Single Mom

by Robin Kaluahine

Survival Mode Was My Normal

I didn't grow up dreaming of becoming a single mom with four kids, two jobs, and running on fast food and fumes. But life rarely goes according to plan.

I was too busy surviving—juggling school events, night shifts, and overdue bills—to think about eating well or taking care of myself. I didn't exercise. I didn't sleep. I lived paycheck to paycheck.

In my late 20s, I went to college while pregnant with my third child, raising two others, and working two jobs. I was exhausted and constantly questioning if I was doing enough—or if I even could. We were so poor that we picked up cans and bottles to buy groceries or gas.

But I kept going. Not because it was easy—but because I believed a better future had to be possible. And I believed I could create it.

That experience taught me something powerful:
You don't have to have it all figured out to take the next step.
You just have to move forward—even when it's hard, even when the outcome is unknown.

The Turning Point

Eventually, I remarried—and found myself in an even worse situation. One morning, I discovered my estranged husband had emptied my personal bank account. I had four kids, a full-time job, and just $1.54 to my name—with two weeks until payday.

No backup. No safety net. No one to call.
So I did what I always did: I figured it out. My grit and determination got us through.

That was the beginning of my transformation—not just financially, but physically, emotionally, and spiritually.

Healing More Than Finances

For years, I believed exhaustion was just part of being a mom. That extra weight? Normal. Brain fog, joint pain, cravings? Just aging, right?

But I was living in survival mode. I did everything for my kids—but nothing for me.
And if I'm honest, I didn't believe I deserved more.
I had spent so long in relationships where I was made to feel small and worthless. I questioned my value. I let insecurity steal my voice and vision.

Then I watched my mother's health decline—complications from unmanaged diabetes, surgeries, and a life cut shorter than it had to be. I saw my future in her path, and I didn't like where it was headed.

That was my wake-up call.

If I didn't take care of myself, I might not be here to enjoy the future I was working so hard to build.

What I Did Differently

I had determination, grit, and the will to rewrite my story. I made small, realistic changes:

- Swapped frozen meals for real food
- Walked for 10 minutes a day
- Learned how blood sugar and inflammation drained my energy
- Found natural supplements that worked
- And eventually, I built a business to help other women do the same

I didn't just change my habits.

I changed my identity.

I went from surviving... to thriving.

What I'd Tell My Younger Self (and You)

You are not stuck.

You are not your family's past.

Even if you only have $1.54 in your account—your story is far from over.

You don't need a perfect plan.

You just need one bold moment—and the courage to keep going.

Together, We Rise

I look back at that naïve girl who married at 19 and see how far I've come. Today, I help women turn their lives in a new direction—toward health, strength, and financial freedom.

We don't have to stay stuck.

Together, we rise.

Together, we glow.

Together, we can all be Million Dollar Moms.

Connect With Robin

www.facebook.com/elaines.attic

@robinkaluahine.com

SHELLEY HINES, RN, MSN

☿

She Rises in Wellness

- A nurse with passion for soul-filled living that includes the sacred Feminine Divine.
- Globally serving women for 30 years privately and in groups.
- Offering soul, mind, body solutions.
- Deepen your connection to your own ease.
- Unblock stuck areas to improve focus and flow in your life.
- Lifestyle Consulting, Evolutionary Astrology, Reiki, & Intentional Creativity(R) to support you in personal growth.
- Join the many women now choosing to be heard, seen and Rise in Wellness!

56SHINES@GMAIL.COM

WWW.SHELLEYHINES.COM

Fierce & Fearless Magazine

Unleash Your Inner Strength and Confidence Today

Explore inspiring stories that empower you to embrace your **fierce, fearless** self.

FIERCE & FEARLESS

JUNE 2025

DARE TO **LEAD** WITHOUT HESITATION WITHIN

LIGHT REIGNS **WITHIN HER**

POWER BURNS WITHIN
Every bold woman dares greatly, shapes destiny, and leads unshaken.

UNLEASH BOLD MIND. BRAVE HEART.

CIARA LEWIS
Empowering women to rise, lead, and redefine their futures.

Secure your spot today for our next issue.

Contact: kllconsultingllc@gmail.com or 606-767-5023

PerfumeCo Africa is a South African Company That's Making Waves in the Fragrance Industry

by Thembi Mokgadi

PerfumeCo Africa is a South African company that's making waves in the fragrance industry. Founded by Bathabile, the company aims to empower individuals from disadvantaged communities by providing them with training and resources to start their own perfume businesses [1].

Mission and Values

PerfumeCo Africa's mission is to be a leading fragrance brand that offers high-quality, affordable perfumes inspired by designer brands. They prioritize local manufacturing and offer distribution opportunities and franchise models. Their unique approach to entrepreneurship focuses on making business accessible to those who may not have the means to start big, emphasizing a willingness to learn and a passion for growth [2].

Impact and Success Stories

The company has already made a significant impact, with many participants running profitable perfume businesses and supporting their families. Thandi, a single mother from Soweto, is a notable success story. She joined PerfumeCo Africa in 2022 and now sells perfumes to support her children and pay for their education. "I never thought I could own a business," Thandi says, "But Bathabile and PerfumeCo gave me the tools to make it happen"

Connect With Thembi

www.tiktok.com/@thembisilemokgadi
www.facebook.com/thembi.m.mokgadi

Finding Spiritual Balance in the Fast Lane

by Shelley Hines

In a world that glorifies hustle, performance, and the never-ending to-do list, many women find themselves constantly in motion. For those of us who are mothers, grandmothers, artists, and authors, the pace can be overwhelming. We run businesses (often solo) whilst we give, create -even give birth, inspire, and nurture—but often at the cost of our own spiritual grounding. In my classes I use a Chinese proverb that says, "If you heal the soul, the mind and body will heal," Wisdom for navigating a full and healthy life. When the soul is well, the mind clears, the body follows suit, and life begins to feel authentic!

The Risk of Losing Authenticity

In the whirlwind of responsibilities, it's easy to slip into patterns of behavior that do not reflect our true nature. We may say "yes" out of obligation. Smiling when we're exhausted and say, 'I'm fine.' Showing up for others but often forgetting to show up for ourselves we fall out of balance. This disconnection from our true self may seem harmless at first, but over time, it leads to spiritual depletion.

Authenticity is not a luxury—it's the anchor that keeps us balanced and rooted in who we are. Without it, we risk burnout, creative blocks, fatigue, and emotional withdrawal. We may continue to function, but our spirit dims. Our work becomes mechanical, our relationships strain, and our inner world may be neglected. Symptoms are whispering, but who is listening? Would you like to learn more about sacred self-care?

Creating Sacred Space in a Busy Life

Spiritual balance doesn't require grand gestures or long hours of solitude, just conscious intentions. It calls for being in the present moment and begins in the small moments of a few deep, quiet breaths before the day begins or when conflict arises. A walk in nature, a whispered prayer, or time spent journaling or listening to calming music is a good start. I believe setting intentions to create the life we want is crucial to successful, healthy living. I have found Evolutionary Astrology (a map) and Intentional Creativity® (magic pens and brushes) to be amazing tools for centering, self-discovery, and healing.

Small acts become sacred pauses; like tending an altar for reflections. We meet our inner lives that allow movements from reactivity to intention, from exhaustion to renewal, and from blocks to creativity and hope.

The Art of Living an Aligned Life

We are all Co-creators with Spirit. One need not be an artist or author to begin creating from a centered place that infuses your work with depth and resonance. When we are aligned and in flow we are unstoppable. As mothers, grandmothers, and entrepreneurs we can model spiritual balance and demonstrate our powerful legacies. When living in alignment, our outer life reflects our inner truth. We move through the world with more clarity, compassion, and joy. Learn self-care from your own authentic intelligence, your internal wisdom! Let me show you how discovering it, and listen to it, enhances your personal and business life with increasing creative ease and flow.

I remember a bumper sticker cautioning, 'Don't drive faster than your angels can fly.' The fast lane is not inherently wrong. But to traverse it well, we must bring our clear intentions with us. It is then we learn to move at the speed of grace, not just the speed of demands and other's timelines. Healing the soul is not selfish—it's a sacred imperative. Remember, when the soul is healed, the mind and body will follow!

About the Author: Shelley Hines is a Registered Nurse, Founder of She Rises in Wellness Women's Retreats, a Pastoral Evolutionary Astrologer, and student of Mary Magdalene. Serving women for over 30 years in the Pacific Northwest and globally, she is currently authoring a creative nonfiction about her call to study Magdalene archetypes in astrology. Her passion is teaching about faith, creativity, astrology, and the art of living authentically

Connect With Shelley
www.shelleyhines.com
www.facebook.com/groups/magdalenesociety
www.facebook.com/56Shines

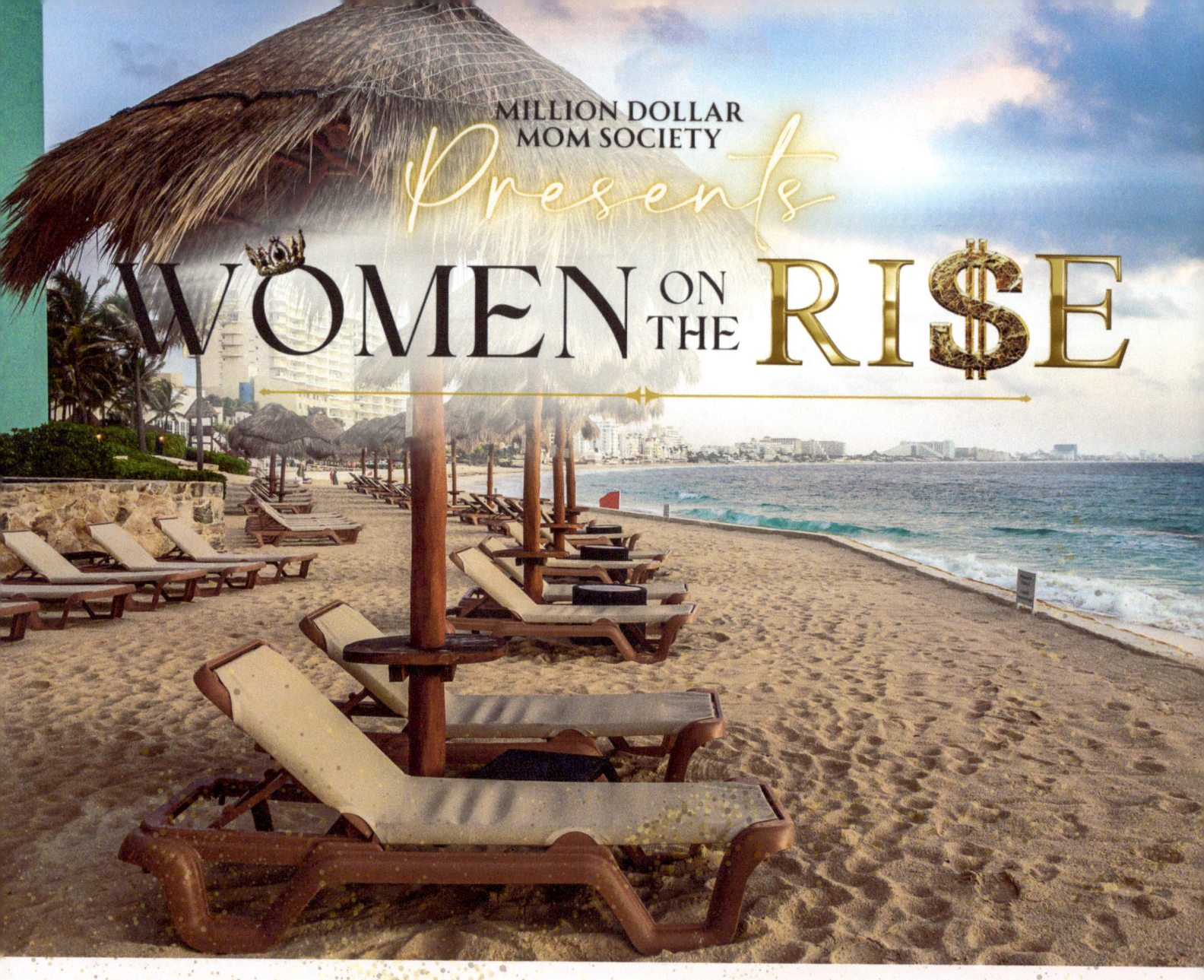

BECOME A SPONSOR OF WOMEN ON THE RISE

**TV SHOW RETREAT MASTERMIND |
NOVEMBER 9–12, 2025 | LAGUNA BEACH**

Your Brand. Global Stage. Unforgettable Impact.

This is not your typical sponsorship opportunity.

Imagine your company being aligned with a high-end, media-covered luxury mastermind filmed for a docu-series airing on **Apple TV and major TV streaming platforms** —alongside elite women entrepreneurs, bestselling authors, and powerhouse speakers like **Forbes Riley**.

We're inviting a select number of brand partners to step into the spotlight and elevate their visibility, influence, and impact in front of a curated audience of high-net-worth women and industry leaders.

As a sponsor, you'll receive:

- Brand placement across event media & red carpet interviews
- On-camera mentions and behind-the-scenes exposure
- Direct access to influential decision-makers & business owners
- Speaking opportunities and product placements (varies by tier)
- A chance to align your brand with purpose, prestige, and power

Whether you want to be seen as a Gold, Diamond, or Platinum Partner, each tier includes increasing visibility, exclusive access, and unforgettable brand moments.

Ready to Position Your Brand Where Influence Meets Luxury?

www.milliondollarmom.org/womenontherise

'From Waiting to Awekening, It's Your Time to Come Alive'

by Michelle Padgett

Awaken the Dreamer Within You

Do you remember the time when your dreams were vivid — when your heart leaped at the thought of a new adventure, the possibility of taking a bold step, and living a life you were truly excited about? Maybe you dreamed of starting a business, traveling the world, writing your story, or creating something that would leave a lasting mark. Perhaps you longed to live with deeper purpose, to build a strong family, or to become the woman you always knew you were meant to be.

But life has a way of layering responsibilities over our dreams.
Schedules grow heavy, and expectations weigh down the soul.
Little by little, often without even realizing it, you tuck those childhood visions and deep inspirations into the quiet corners of your heart.

You tell yourself, "One day soon, I'll come back to them."
"Maybe when things slow down, maybe when I'm stronger, maybe when someone finally believes in me."
And so, day after day, season after season, those beautiful dreams stay tucked away, gathering dust.

Here's the beautiful truth I want you to hear today:

The dreams you buried are still there, Just waiting for you to believe again.

Your dreams don't die because life gets busy.
They don't even disappear because time has passed.
Your dreams remain within you, as vibrant as the day they were born — patient, persistent, and powerful.

You have not missed your chance. You are not too late.
In fact, you are wiser now. Stronger. More equipped to achieve these lifetime goals.

The very journey that made you wonder if you were too far behind has been preparing you all along for what's next.

God didn't place those desires in your heart by accident.
The passions, the visions, and quiet longings — they are all seeds of purpose, planted by His own hand.
You may have forgot them, but He never did.

This is your season to awaken the dreamer within you.
You don't have to do everything all at once and You don't need to have it all figured out.

All you need is to take one brave step forward to pursue your dreams.

Maybe it's writing the first page of the book you once dreamed of.
Maybe it's signing up for the class you've always wanted to take.
Maybe it's simply carving out sacred time to dream big, create, and hope again.

Each small step is a victory and every act of believing again declares to your soul and to the world: My story isn't over yet.

Let go of the fear that says it's too late.

Silence the comparisons that whisper you're a failure.
Dismiss the shame that says you should have already arrived.
Why? You are right on time for the destiny that God designed just for you.

Dear woman of courage and hope, hear this:

The world still needs you.
Your voice carries a unique imprint that only you can give.
Your family still needs your love.
Your calling still needs your yes.

It's not about chasing perfection or being perfect.
It's about showing up — offering the most precious gift you have: yourself.

Within you lies treasure — gold, silver, jewels — in the form of your talents, skills, and dreams.
And as you grow, mature, and step forward, you're becoming the very best version of you.

So take that step.
Trust God — the Farmer of your dreams — to guide and provide.
Beneath those layers of daily life, and doubt, The flames of your passion still burns.
Your voice is still powerful.
Your purpose is still alive.

And it's waiting, not for perfect conditions, but for your wholehearted, courageous YES.

"She believed again, and now is her time to bloom."
- VictoriousMichelle

Connect With Michelle

www.VictoriousMichelle.com
@victoriousmichelle
www.vision-star.com
www.facebook.com/mchllpdgtt

Become a Managing Partner

she wins
W O M E N ' S   N E T W O R K

Join a global Movement of Visionary Women
50+ Chapters. Transformative Community. Unlimited Growth.

WHAT'S INCLUDED

- 40% commission on memberships + event bonuses
- Leadership training, toolkits & ongoing support
- VIP access to retreats, masterminds & more

Join for just

$297

Application Fee (paid only after acceptance)

www.shewinswomensnetwork.com

What If Your Child's Potential to Lead Is Never Discovered?

HERO KIDS LEAD

An empowering 9-week leadership course helping every child discover the superhero within!

**Ages:
6 to 12 Welcome!**

CONTACT INFORMATION:

www.herokidslead.com

REGISTER NOW!

WATCH YOUR CHILD GROW IN:

- ✓ **Public Speaking**
- ✓ **Team-Building**
- ✓ **Identity & Self-Worth**
- ✓ **Confidence**
- ✓ **Self-Discipline**
- ✓ **Leadership**

Global Women of Impact:
Where Cultures Connect, Leaders Rise & Purposeful Change Begins

by Anisa Crespo

At Global Women of Impact (GWOI), we believe there's extraordinary power when women from every walk of life unite—not just in conversation, but in collaboration. As we step into this new season of opportunity, we're thrilled to launch new programs, initiatives, and global connections designed to empower women everywhere to lead, rise, and thrive.

But before we share what's ahead, we want to take a moment to reflect on what makes this mission so sacred—and why it matters more than ever in today's divided world.

The Heartbeat of GWOI: Unity Through Diversity

GWOI was born out of a desire to bridge cultural gaps and strengthen unity among women from all ethnicities. Whether you're in Morocco, Miami, or Mexico City, our message is clear: your story, your voice, and your leadership matter.

Our founder, Mona Loubna Cherkaoui, brings more than 30 years of international business experience to the table, and her vision is deeply rooted in her multicultural upbringing. A Moroccan woman who made the United States her home, Mona grew up with a deep reverence for community, connection, and inclusion.

"I've spent my life studying cultures—not just observing their customs, but understanding their core," Mona shares. "It's this curiosity and compassion that inspired me to bring women together from around the world to create impact, leadership, and legacy."

Our mission is simple yet powerful:
- To nurture a global community of women who uplift, educate, and empower each other through collaboration and collective action.
- To break down societal and cultural barriers so every woman, no matter her background, can lead with confidence, be seen, and create change.

We are not just a network—we are a movement of changemakers.

Breaking Barriers, Building Bridges

At GWOI, we challenge the status quo. We ask hard questions. We listen deeply. And we take action. We believe women don't need to fit into outdated molds to be successful. We believe in redefining leadership through empathy, inclusivity, and cultural intelligence.

Through our culturally responsive programs, mentorship circles, and global events, we create environments where women feel safe to be authentic, inspired to dream bigger, and equipped to lead.

Our motto is simple:
When one woman rises, we all rise.

What's New: Our 2025 Global Launch & Upcoming Programs

We are proud to unveil several new initiatives that will shape the future of Global Women of Impact:

1. SHE Echoes Globally (Speaker Series + Summit Platform)

A global stage for women to share their stories of adversity, achievement, and action. SHE Echoes spotlights women who are amplifying their voice to create change. Whether you're a first-time speaker or a seasoned storyteller, this platform honors your truth and empowers your journey.

2. Coffee with a Leader

This is not your average networking chat. Each intimate online session features a female executive, entrepreneur, or visionary leader sharing tangible lessons and mentorship in a conversational format. Think of it as leadership over lattes—raw, real, and rich in wisdom.

3. The Global Business Lounge

Our newest hub for women entrepreneurs and executives looking to expand their business beyond borders. Members receive access to global expansion workshops, strategic partnerships, cross-cultural coaching, and market insights designed to help you scale your vision worldwide.

4. SiStarships Mentorship Program

We pair emerging women leaders with experienced mentors from diverse industries and countries. This isn't just about skill-building—it's about creating legacy relationships, opening doors, and raising the bar for future generations of women.

5. Leadership Accelerator & Mastermind Cohorts

Launching this year, our intensive 12-week leadership incubator will guide women through high-level training in negotiation, cultural intelligence, ethical leadership, and entrepreneurial scaling. If you're ready to lead on a global stage, this is for you.

Why This Matters Now

In a world where division dominates the headlines, the need for women-led unity, collaboration, and courageous leadership has never been greater. The challenges women face are complex and intersectional—affected by culture, geography, economics, and more.

At GWOI, we don't believe in a one-size-fits-all approach. Instead, we ask:

- How can we honor each woman's unique experience while building a collective movement?
- How can we create programs that are as culturally inclusive as they are transformational?
- How can we ensure that no woman is left behind, no matter her location, background, or circumstances?

Our answer: Education. Empowerment. And collective action. We provide real-world tools, cultural fluency, and access to global leadership circles—because we know you're not just meant to survive... you're meant to lead.

From the Desk of Our President, Anisa Crespo

"As a mom, business coach, and leader, I know how hard it can be to navigate both professional ambition and cultural expectations," shares GWOI President Anisa Crespo. "But I also know this: when women are given the right support, mentorship, and platform, there's nothing we can't do."

Anisa's leadership is rooted in her commitment to faith, family, and financial freedom for women. She brings practical tools, mindset mentorship, and her own lived experiences into the programs she co-creates with Mona and the GWOI board.

"This isn't about perfection—it's about progress. We're here to empower the woman raising babies and building dreams. The woman starting over after divorce or burnout. The woman navigating international markets and motherhood at the same time. This is your tribe," says Anisa.

The Global Impact Starts With You

We're not waiting for the world to change—we're creating the change together. As we step into this Summer of Success, we invite you to:

- Join one of our global programs or masterminds
- Apply to be a SHE Echoes speaker or host a cultural event in your city
- Mentor a sister or apply to be mentored through Sistarships
- Show up boldly, share your truth, and lead with love

Because at Global Women of Impact, you belong. Your leadership matters. And your voice echoes farther than you know.

Final Word

This is more than an organization—it's a global sisterhood. A home for dreamers and doers. A community where boundaries are broken and bridges are built. A space where you don't have to choose between heritage and leadership, motherhood and ambition, success and sisterhood.

Together, we rise. Together, we thrive.
And together, we will shape a better world—one woman, one story, one mission at a time.

Ready to Be the Change? Join the Movement.

Whether you're an aspiring leader, seasoned changemaker, or simply a woman with a heart for impact—you belong here.

Become a member of Global Women of Impact and gain access to world-class mentorship, global leadership programs, business expansion opportunities, and a culturally rich sisterhood that will support you every step of the way.

Your voice matters. Your leadership is needed. Your time is now.

Visit https://gwoiOrlando.org to join us today and take your place among the women shaping the future of our world—together.

Welcome to Global Women of Impact.

Connect With Us

www.gwoiOrlando.org
www.facebook.com/GWOI.NET
www.facebook.com/groups/1109491926275588

How to Successfully Make It Through Your Season of Healing

by Angela Turpin

Despite what may have been depicted for women in the past, healing is not all sunshine and rainbows. If you add the layer of healing from sexual abuse, even the idea seems like the pit of hell you must climb out of.

What if you're a woman, a mom, and or a business owner who suddenly remembered she had this traumatic experience in her life? Or maybe you might have been ignoring it and pretending like it doesn't impact you.

I have experienced all of the above. Pretending that it did not impact me or my life. (I thought it was normal that I did not want to hug people.) I also had a flashback of childhood abuse almost 27 years later. Even then, I did not think it impacted my life. Until I was pregnant 2 years later by a man, I had only known for 2 weeks!

Since my pregnancy, I have spent time, energy, space, and money on healing from sexual abuse. Abuse as a child and two times as an adult. I can tell you that it was not pretty as I was led to believe. However, it is possible to come out of your healing season feeling fulfilled, successful, and like it was all worth it.

This is how it's done.

1. Stop meditating. I know this was probably your nonnegotiable in your morning routine. But if you are a woman who just remembered or is finally facing it, you're probably learning that meditation feels like it did when you first started. Chaotic and unsafe! Like you can't get your mind to shut off! You can walk with music on. This will help you silence your mind. Until you release without reliving, your mind will be a battleground. This is why in my 1:1 work we focus on releasing without reliving so you can get back to meditating.

2. Connect with your body. This will be the most critical thing that you can do. You may notice that you're totally disconnected from your body. You might try to connect with your body through breathwork or meditation. However, there's something that you can do that will slow you down and shift yourself into the present moment more often which is more powerful over time. It's noticed with your senses. Notice something that sounds amazing, that tastes great, that looks beautiful, smells delicious. This slows you down, connects you to your body, and brings you to the present daily!

3. Acknowledge your victim mindset. You might have cringed a bit. I get that. As a woman who wants to be successful in everything you do, you already know that the victim mindset keeps you stuck and stagnant. In the case of healing from sexual abuse/assault, you must acknowledge and accept that you were the victim. If you don't, you will fight against your healing. Quite honestly you won't feel as successful as you would like. When you acknowledge and accept, your whole world will change, it will be like seeing everything from a different lens. Now, you are not meant to stay here. But you must accept that is part of your story!

This is how you can come out of your healing successful, fulfilled and ready to take on anything. Healing is not easy, but it is worth it. When you heal from this kind of trauma everything else falls into place!

Cheers to your successful season!

Connect With Angela

www.transformwithangela.com
www.instagram.com/transformwithangela

The M.O.M Method

Magnetize   Optimize   Monetize

The MOM Method is your ultimate roadmap to building a profitable business without sacrificing your time, energy, or family life. We'll show you how to attract aligned leads into your Facebook group, craft irresistible offers, and automate your entire sales process. Whether you're just getting started or scaling to six figures, we've got the blueprint to take you there with ease.

You'll walk away with proven frameworks for growing an engaged community, launching high-ticket offers, and building a sustainable offer suite that brings consistent revenue. Plus, we include done-for-you tools, launch-ready templates, and lifetime support so you're never doing it alone. It's time to grow smarter, not harder—with systems that actually work for moms like you.

Nourish to Flourish:
Why Mindful Eating Is the Key to Feeling Better in Your Body and Life

by Linda Bah

In a world where multitasking is the norm and food is often eaten in the car, between meetings, or while wrangling kids, the simple act of eating has become rushed and unconscious. For many women, eating is something that happens while doing three other things—or worse, something to feel guilty about afterward.

But what if the path to better digestion, balanced energy, and food freedom didn't start with another diet... but with awareness?

That's the beauty of mindful eating—a gentle, non-diet approach that invites you to slow down, tune in, and truly enjoy the nourishment your body deserves.

What Is Mindful Eating?

Mindful eating is the practice of paying full attention to your eating experience—your hunger cues, the taste and texture of your food, and how your body feels before, during, and after a meal. It means shifting out of autopilot and into presence, without judgment.

It's not about perfection. It's about intention.

Mindful eating invites us to stop moralizing food as "good" or "bad," and instead explore how different foods make us feel—physically and emotionally.

Why It Matters for Women

For women—especially moms, caregivers, and busy professionals—mindful eating can be a game-changer. Research shows that mindful eating helps reduce emotional eating, improve digestion, and support weight regulation without restriction.

It also lowers stress levels, improves hormonal balance, and increases body satisfaction. In other words, it doesn't just change your plate—it transforms your relationship with food and yourself.

Women who eat mindfully often report:
- Fewer cravings and less emotional eating
- Better digestion and less bloating
- More energy and fewer energy crashes
- A more compassionate, guilt-free attitude toward food

Easy Mindful Eating Tips & Hacks

You don't need to overhaul your entire lifestyle to start. Here are some easy ways to bring mindful eating into your everyday routine:

1. Pause Before You Eat:

Take a deep breath. Ask yourself: "Am I truly hungry, or am I bored, stressed, or tired?" That pause builds awareness.

2. Sit Down (Even for 5 Minutes):

Eating while standing or on the go can lead to overeating. Sit down, even if it's just for a few bites.

3. Use All Your Senses:

Notice the color, texture, and aroma of your food. Chew slowly and savor each bite. The more you notice, the more satisSied you'll feel.

4. HALT Before Snacking:

Use the HALT method—Am I Hungry, Angry, Lonely, or Tired? Often, we're feeding an emotion, not a hunger.

5. Start with One Mindful Meal a Day:

Don't try to overhaul every meal. Choose one meal a day to be distraction-free and intentional. That's enough to begin shifting your habits.

6. Be Kind to Yourself:

If you overeat or snack mindlessly, don't beat yourself up. Guilt creates stress, and stress fuels the very habits you want to change. Just notice and begin again.

The Bottom Line

You don't need another diet—you need a deeper connection with your body. Mindful eating offers a powerful, sustainable way to nourish yourself from the inside out. It helps you Slourish—not by controlling food, but by understanding your relationship with it.

Whether you're a mom feeding little ones, a busy entrepreneur, or simply a woman trying to feel better in your body, mindful eating is a path back to the joy, energy, and balance you deserve.

So, the next time you sit down to eat, take a breath. Slow down. Tune in. And remember—you are worthy of nourishment, in every sense of the word.

Want to bring mindful eating into your everyday life?

If this message resonates with you and you're ready to feel more in tune with your body, more at peace with food, and more energized in your day-to-day life, let's talk. Together, we'll personalize your journey and turn mindful eating from a concept into a sustainable, life-changing practice. Book a free, no-pressure chat with me today (scan the QR code below) and let's explore what's possible. These spots Sill up quickly, so don't wait to take that Sirst nourishing step—your well- being is worth it.

I am including, for your easy reference, a free tool that you can use to help you navigate through mindful eating.

https://4foldlifehealthcoaching.
my.canva.site/dagiauzlxok

Connect With Linda

www.instagram.com/4foldlifehealthcoaching
www.facebook.com/groups/306664992198005
www.lindabah.juiceplus.com/us/en-us
www.us.fullscript.com/welcome/lindabah

From Hustle to Harmony:
Turning Your Vision into Reality

by BreAnna Finco

I'll never forget the moment I saw that picture. My son, Addison, had drawn our family—everyone smiling, everyone together—but at the very bottom of the page, in a small box, there I was. When I asked him why he had put me there, his answer shattered my heart: "Because Mommy is working." That single sentence hit me like a freight train. My heart sank, and tears filled my eyes. At that moment, I realized I was chasing success so aggressively that I'd lost sight of why I started this journey in the first place: to create freedom, fulfillment, and lasting memories with the people I love most.

Back then, before creating FInCo, I had fallen into the hustle trap. I believed constant work was necessary to satisfy my clients, colleagues, and business partners. Every late night, every missed dinner, and every "just one more email" silently robbed me of precious family time and genuine fulfillment. Success felt hollow because the people who mattered most weren't experiencing it with me.

That moment of clarity sparked a dramatic shift and set me on a journey to discover a better way—a way that didn't force me to choose between business success and being present for my family. Over time, through lessons learned the hard way, I developed the Vision-to-Reality (V2R) Framework. It became my solution to achieving harmony, balance, and true, meaningful success without the hustle.

The V2R Framework begins by clarifying your vision—not just professionally, but personally. What do you truly want your life to look like? How do you want to feel each day? Gaining crystal-clear clarity sets the foundation for intentional, aligned action.

Next is strategy. Once your vision is clear, you build a focused, strategic plan centered on impactful steps and sustainable growth. No more scattershot efforts or endless busywork—just purposeful actions that directly move you toward your goals.

Finally, you streamline your budget and systems. By optimizing your finances and embracing simple automation, you reclaim valuable personal and family time. Instead of working harder, you start working smarter, ensuring your business supports your ideal lifestyle.

The true power of the V2R Framework is its impact in real life. One of my clients, a dedicated physical trainer, came to me overwhelmed by the demands of her business. She had big dreams but felt stuck in the hustle cycle. Together, we implemented the V2R Framework, beginning with a strategic rebrand that elevated her visibility and attracted her ideal clients. Through careful launch planning and meticulous financial tracking, she watched her business transform. Now, she's confidently moving toward her Financial Independence Number, achieving tangible milestones without sacrificing her personal well-being or valuable family time.

If you're tired of the hustle and ready to create true harmony between your entrepreneurial dreams and the life you cherish, the Vision-to-Reality Framework is your solution.

Ready to finally turn YOUR vision into reality—without sacrificing what matters most? Scan the QR code now to download your FREE Vision-to-Reality (V2R) Framework and begin creating harmony, balance, and true success today!

SCAN ME

Connect With BreAnna

www.breannafinco.com
www.facebook.com/breanna.finco
www.instagram.com/thejoielab
www.createjoie.com

LEGACY IN THE MAKING: REAL TALK. REAL RESULTS.

Watch Legacy Makers with Natosha Navarro & Anisa Crespo as they share how they left the 9-to-5 grind, launched powerful businesses, and built a life of freedom on their own terms. From military service and motherhood to six-figure success, their journey is both relatable and revolutionary.

Get the real story behind their rise—how they crafted high-ticket offers, grew online communities from the ground up, and mastered the art of scaling without burnout. This episode is your playbook for turning passion into profit.

TUNE IN NOW!

www.legacymakerstv.com/anisa-crespo-and-natosha-navarro

MILLION DOLLAR
Mom Society

Natosha Navarro

Anisa Crespo

Magnetize and Monetize your Market Podcast

Calling all ambitious women! Tune in to Magnetize and Monetize Your Market, hosted by the powerhouse duo Anisa Crespo & Natosha Navarro, co-founders of Million Dollar Mom Society. Get ready for mindset shifts, marketing strategies, and manifestation techniques to attract your dream clients and build a thriving business. Listen now and start scaling your empire!

Listen on
Apple Podcasts

https://podcasts.apple.com/us/podcast/magnetize-and-monetize-your-market-podcast/id1786618997